FISH TALES

By Nat Segaloff & Paul Erickson   Illustrated by Bob Barner

Sterling Publishing Co., Inc.   New York

Library of Congress Cataloging-in-Publication Data

Segaloff, Nat.
  Fish tales / by Nat Segaloff & Paul Erickson; illustrated by Bob
Barner.
    p.   cm.
  Summary: Describes the physical characteristics, habitat, and
behavior of different types of fish.
  ISBN 0-8069-7322-6. — ISBN 0-8069-7323-4 (lib. bdg.)
  1. Fishes—Juvenile literature. [1. Fishes.] I. Erickson, Paul
A. II. Barner, Bob, ill. III. Title.
QL617.2.S43   1990
597—dc20   89-26279
                                                   CIP
                                                    AC

Copyright © 1990 by the New England Aquarium
Published by Sterling Publishing Co., Inc.
387 Park Avenue South, New York, N.Y. 10016
Distributed in Canada by Sterling Publishing
℅ Canadian Manda Group, P.O. Box 920, Station U
Toronto, Ontario, Canada M8Z 5P9
Distributed in Great Britain and Europe by Cassell PLC
Artillery House, Artillery Row, London SW1P 1RT, England
Distributed in Australia by Capricorn Ltd.
P.O. Box 665, Lane Cove, NSW 2066
Manufactured in the United States of America
All rights reserved
Sterling ISBN 0-8069-7322-6 Trade
              7323-4 Library

Dedicated to the memory of
Jack McKenney, diver and un-
derwater cinematographer, who
inspired our appreciation for
the world of water.

Thanks to Dennis Campbell
who helped cultivate the idea,
to Sandra Goldfarb for her
guiding spirit, to Les Kaufman
and John Dayton for ideas, sup-
port, and advice, and to Bob
Barner for his fine work and
commitment to the project.

Fish Tales is published to cele-
brate the diversity of life in the
oceans, with the hope that it
will be preserved for future
generations.

The New England Aquarium is
a private, nonprofit institution
dedicated to making known the
World of Water through education, research, conservation, and
the exhibition of aquatic life.

New England Aquarium

Imagine a journey back through time, more than three-and-a-half billion years ago, to an ancient sea. Here, chemical building blocks come together, and the process of life begins.

Over the eons, plants and animals develop into an immense number of forms. Some flourish. Others vanish. Eventually a group of swimming animals with backbones appears: the first fishes.

EARLY FISH

SEA

LAKES

RIVERS

STREAM

DESERT WATERHOLE

ANTARCTIC OCEAN

Fishes continue to evolve for the next 500 million years. Today, more than 25,000 kinds of fishes live throughout the waters of the world. They thrive in the depths of the sea and in high mountain lakes, in raging rivers and in mountain streams, in the frigid Antarctic ocean as well as in desert waterholes of 110 degrees Fahrenheit.

DEVILS HOLE PUPFISH

In the fish world, the variety seems endless. Some fishes are the size of your smallest finger-nail even when they are fully grown adults. One reaches the length of a subway car. To you, some may look ordinary, others strange, some beautiful, others not-so-beautiful.

Before we introduce you to some fascinating fishes, let's try to answer a basic question. Exactly what is a fish? With many thousands of different kinds swimming around, that's a difficult question to answer. However, there are some general facts we can tell you.

GREAT BARRACUDA

STINGRAY

BLUE STRIPED GRUNT

GREEN MORAY EEL

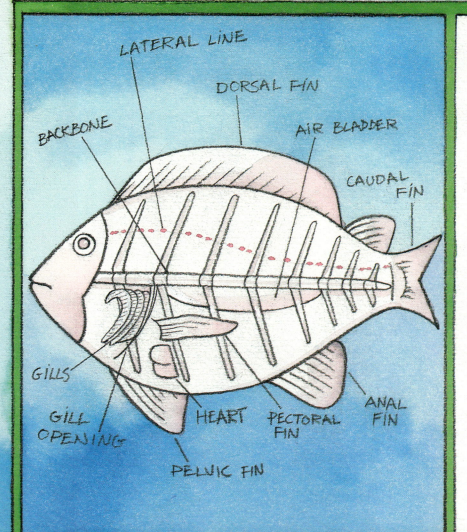

LATERAL LINE

DORSAL FIN

BACKBONE

AIR BLADDER

CAUDAL FIN

GILLS

GILL OPENING

HEART

PECTORAL FIN

ANAL FIN

PELVIC FIN

Fishes have backbones, and *most* have jaws for eating and gills for breathing. Typically their bodies are covered with scales, and their limbs are usually in the form of fins. For buoyancy they have inflatable or oil-filled swim bladders. Almost all have two-chambered hearts as compared to the human heart which has four. Fishes have well developed senses of sight, touch, smell, taste, and hearing. They also have a sixth sense: the lateral line system. This consists of tiny canals that span from head to tail, just under the skin, one on each side of the body. Each canal contains microscopic hairs that detect the movements of water around the fish.

But there are some fishes that don't completely fit our model. The lamprey, like its prehistoric ancestors, is jawless. Sharks, skates, and rays have no bones at all in their bodies. Their skeletons are made of cartilage, the material that forms the tip of your nose. Ever hear the expression "like a fish out of water"? Meet the mudskipper. This fish can move around on land, using special gills and throat tissue that absorb oxygen from air.

LAMPREY

MUDSKIPPER

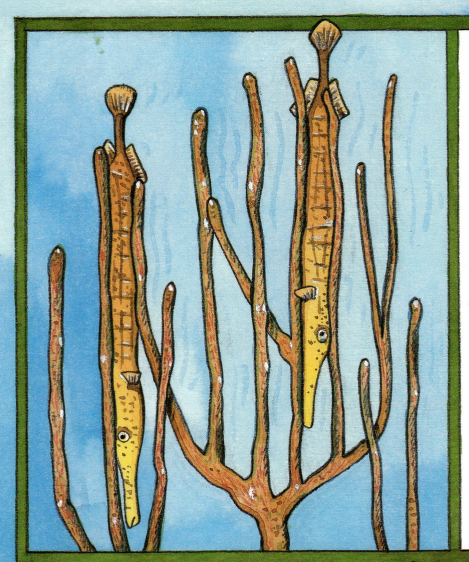

Every kind of fish has a design that helps it stay alive in its natural surroundings. But regardless of where they live, all fishes face the same challenges. To survive and reproduce they have to eat, avoid being eaten, and find a mate, just like the trumpet fish hiding here in the soft coral.

Fishes meet their day-to-day challenges through a remarkable array of colors, shapes, and devices. Let's take the plunge and see some of them, starting with an animal with shocking table manners.

TRUMPET FISH

Beneath the jungle canopy of the Brazilian rain forest, the Amazon River winds through South America to the sea. In this tropical world there exists one of nature's miracles, the electric eel. While all animals, even people, give off small amounts of electricity, this fish generates enough power to give you a very painful shock.

ORCHID

Using organs that work like thousands of flashlight batteries lined end-to-end, the electric eel creates a low voltage field around its body, which helps it tell if anything comes near. If that "anything" is a potential meal, such as a small fish, the eel unleashes a powerful electric shock for some fast food.

ELECTRIC EEL

11

Sharing these waters with the electric eel are some fishes with legendary appetites: piranhas. At least 20 kinds of piranhas live in the inland waters of South America. Using strong jaws and razor-sharp teeth, they're capable of slicing chunks of flesh from other animals. Although piranhas usually eat fish, including other piranhas, they also dine on fruits and seeds that drop from trees.

CARNIVORE PIRANHA (RED-BELLIED)

Do piranhas attack people? Once in a while, but most of the legends you have heard just aren't true. South Americans often work and play in the same waters where piranhas swim, usually without any problems. But piranhas are unpredictable. Some kinds are more dangerous than others, and their danger may be even greater during their breeding season.

VEGETARIAN PIRANHA (PACU)

It's not so easy to spot a meal in the muddy waters of a rain forest. It's also a challenge in the deep sea, a mile beneath the surface, in almost total darkness. Here, food is scarce. When a fish finally finds something to eat, it had better get the biggest bite possible, or go hungry for quite some time.

Prowling these deep waters are some of the world's most fearsome-looking creatures, including the sabertoothed viperfish. Like many of its neighbors, it generates a cold light chemically, like a firefly. The viperfish lures prey with a glowing spot on its top fin, snaps its jaws shut, and traps its meal inside with long, needle-like teeth.

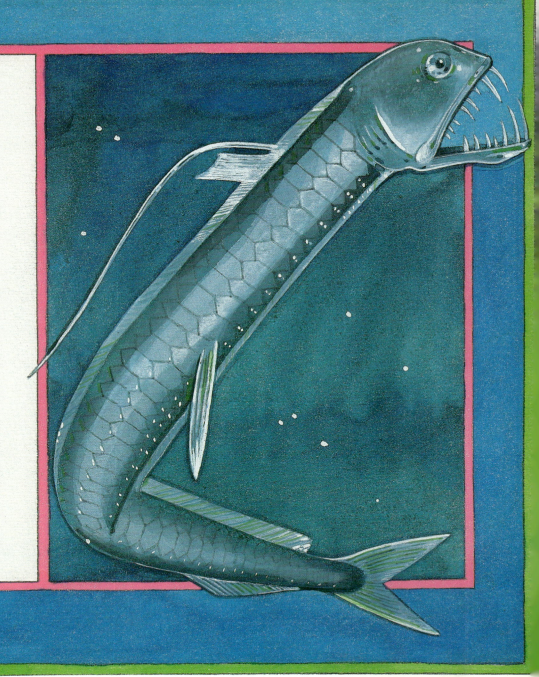

Fishes have special ways of gathering food, but how do fishes avoid becoming food themselves? To eat a fish, first you have to find it. Take a good look. Can you find the fish right in front of you? No, it's not invisible, it's camouflaged. This scorpionfish blends into its surroundings on a coral reef. Predators probably have a difficult time finding this fish.

SCORPIONFISH

Here's a fish that's not using camouflage, but it is protected . . . with built-in armor. When attacked, the porcupinefish inflates with water to form a spiny balloon. Now how many predators would want to swallow that?

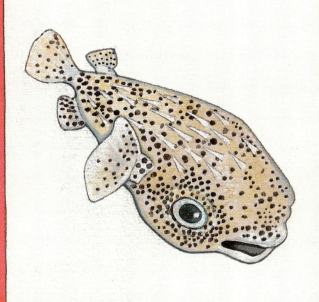

PORCUPINEFISH

Some fishes use chemical warfare for protection. This lionfish injects poison into attackers that come into contact with the venomous fins along its back. The sting is extremely painful, but not usually fatal to people.

LIONFISH

On a slightly more friendly note, meet the clownfish and its bodyguard, a sea anemone. This anemone, a stinging relative of the jellyfish, dines on shrimp and small fishes. Even fishes too large to be seriously harmed by the anemone avoid its stinging tentacles.

CLOWNFISH

Where does the clownfish fit in? Right among the anemone's tentacles! Because predators avoid the stingers, the anemone protects the clownfish which—amazingly—never gets stung itself. Why not? No one is sure, but here's one idea. Like many fishes, clownfish have a slime or mucous coating. Biologists think that a special ingredient in the mucous coating of the fish may keep the anemone's stinging cells from firing.

ANEMONE

Eating and not being eaten are essential for individual fish to survive. But, of course, individuals don't live forever. So if the whole species is to continue, fishes must reproduce. To accomplish this vital task, fishes use a variety of tactics.

The first step is finding a mate. In many species, both males and females advertise with elaborate color schemes. The bright pink square on this male *Anthias* probably attracts a female. Many fishes are sensitive to the colors of their mates, so the mate is easier to find.

Not only sight, but also sound appear to be an important part of fish courtship. This toadfish probably attracts mates with sound generated by vibrating muscles against its swim bladder.

TOADFISH

Many fishes practice what you might call freestyle mating, in which the male and female separately release enormous amounts of sperm and eggs into the same area of the open sea. Fertilization and survival of the young in this way become a matter of chance. A female cod, for example, can lay tens of millions of eggs in its lifetime. If every egg hatched and every young cod survived, the oceans would soon be solid fish. But many eggs never get fertilized, and most of those that do become food for other sea creatures. So, this usually results in just a handful of survivors—just enough to keep the species alive.

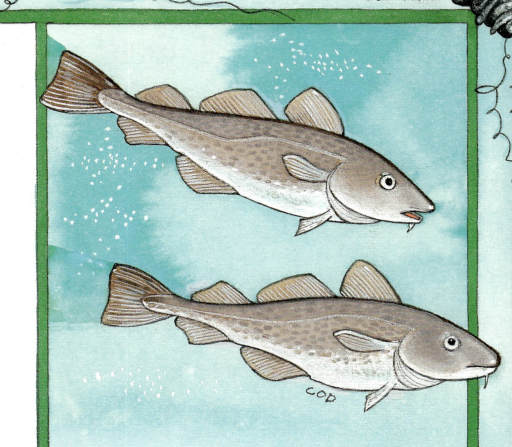

COD

SKATE EGG CASE

For some fishes, mating is a complex affair that can result in strange attachments. Once attracted to the larger female, the male deep sea anglerfish holds on to her with his sharp teeth. Eventually their skins fuse, and their veins and arteries permanently unite. As many as three males may join the same female in this way, supplying sperm, when needed, to externally fertilize the eggs she releases.

Fishes that do not lay as many eggs as the cod or deep sea anglerfish tend their eggs to increase the chances of their offsprings' survival. Sea horses have a unique approach to incubation and fatherhood. The female sea horse lays her eggs in the male's pouch, which is a bit like a kangaroo's. The male fertilizes them as they enter the pouch. About ten days later, he delivers as many as 700 fully formed young into the sea.

The variety of mating processes, protective devices, and feeding methods helps fishes stay alive. And the fishes that are alive today form the latest chapter in a long story—a success story. There are more kinds of fishes than all the amphibians, reptiles, birds, and mammals combined.

SEA HORSE

HAMMERHEAD SHARK

Of the thousands of species of fishes, some simply capture our imaginations more than others. Yell "shark" and two things may happen: You'll either fill a movie theater or clear the water. That's because sharks have a reputation as spectacular eating machines. In most cases their reputation is earned, but normally they eat sea creatures, not people. Most of the roughly 350 known species of sharks are too small, too uninterested, or are too deep in the ocean to bother people.

You might consider sleek, swift beauties like the mako or the blue shark as typical sharks. But some are not so typical.

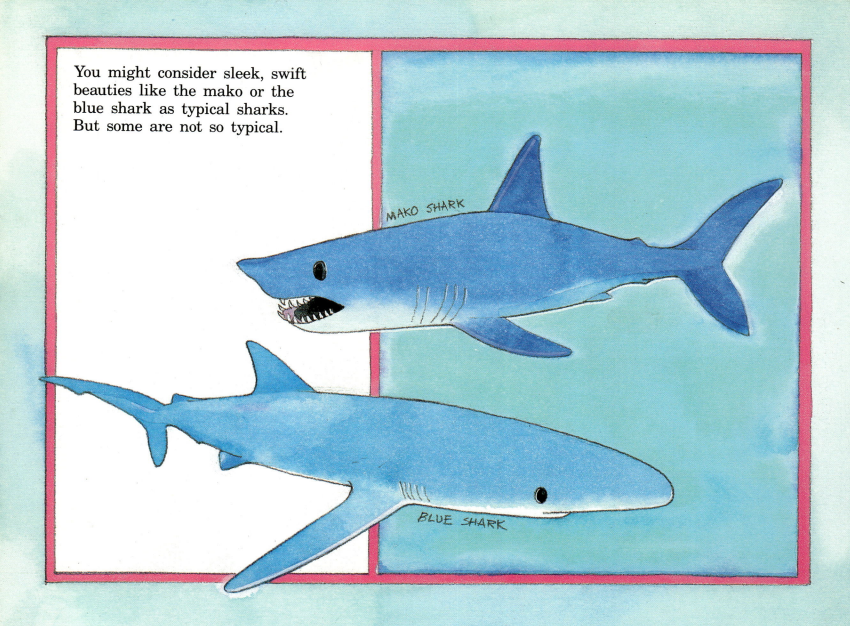

MAKO SHARK

BLUE SHARK

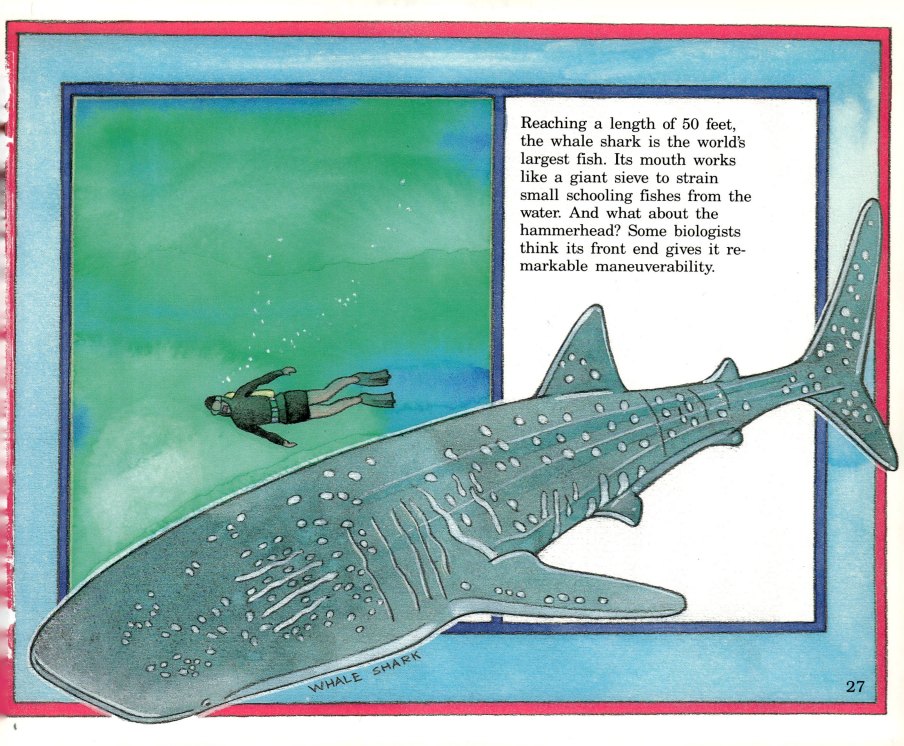

Reaching a length of 50 feet, the whale shark is the world's largest fish. Its mouth works like a giant sieve to strain small schooling fishes from the water. And what about the hammerhead? Some biologists think its front end gives it remarkable maneuverability.

WHALE SHARK

Because sharks have no swim bladder for buoyancy, most of them must either swim or sink. Some, like the nurse shark, lie on the seafloor where they ambush and eat other bottom dwellers.

NURSE SHARK

28

GREAT WHITE SHARK

But when it comes to feeding, here's the expert. It's a fast-moving predator that's a Hollywood star, but many ocean creatures see it as something to avoid: the great white shark.

The great white is one of the largest hunters in the sea—adults are usually 14 to 18 feet long, although they've been reported up to 25.

Using powerful jaws and large teeth with saw-toothed edges, a great white can devour sea mammals as large as seals. Like all sharks and many other fishes, the great white constantly produces new rows of teeth. If the ones in front get dull or fall out—no problem— they'll be replaced as the next row moves forward.

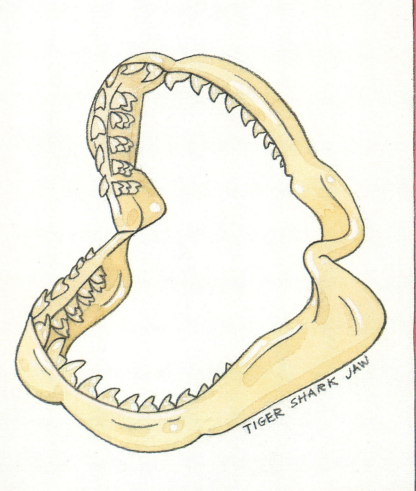

TIGER SHARK JAW

The great white is a dangerous animal, but you'll probably never meet one unless you go shark hunting. And shark attacks on people are so rare that, in most places, the possibility of one shouldn't keep you out of the water. As a matter of fact, sharks are far more often attacked by people than people are by sharks. Does the great white eat people? Yes, but only on rare occasions.

GRAY SEAL

So from big jaws to little jaws, from electric eels to fishes that carry their own lights, and from those that sting to those that sing, in a world mostly covered by water, there are countless fish tales to tell. We've mentioned a few of our favorites, and some may seem unusual.

But remember. No matter how strange a given fish might seem to us, the reason it's here is because it's successful and it survives. Besides, who are we to pass judgment? From their point of view, we might look strange too!

EDUCATION